STAR WARS
EPISODE III
REVENGE OF THE SITH
Music by JOHN WILLIAMS

Project Manager: **Carol Cuellar**
Book Art Layout: **Ernesto Ebanks**
Arranged by **Bill Galliford,**
Ethan Neuburg and **Tod Edmondson**

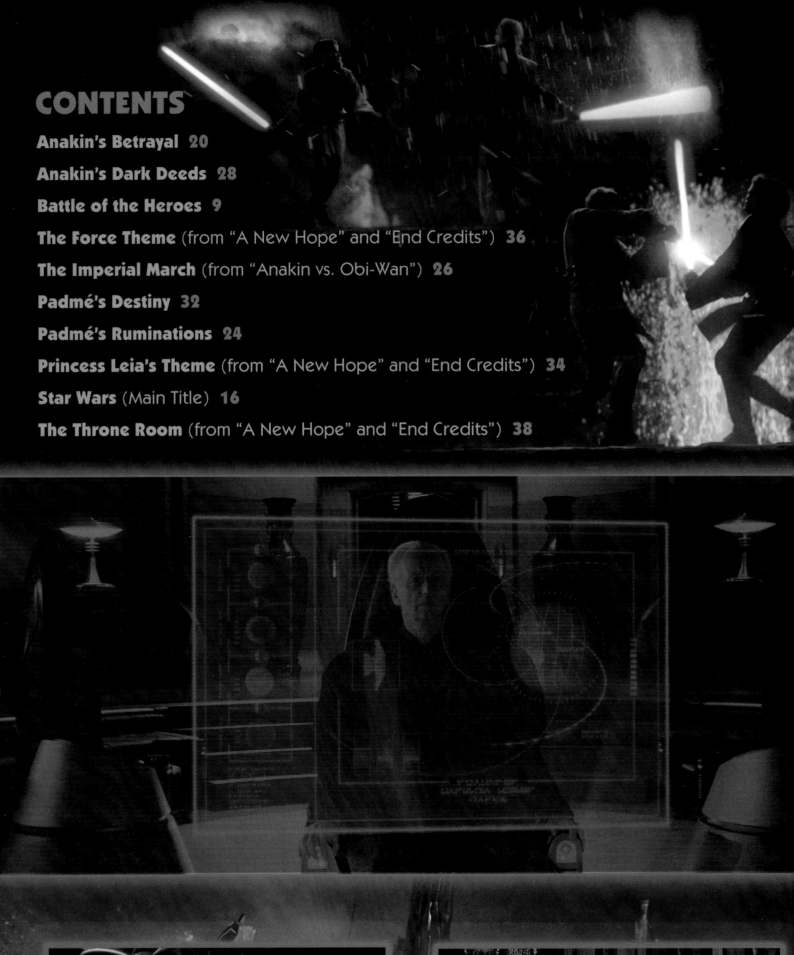

CONTENTS

BATTLE OF THE HEROES

Music by
JOHN WILLIAMS

Maestoso, with great force ($\quad$ = 92)

Battle of the Heroes - 7 - 1
PFM0513

10

12

STAR WARS
(Main Title)

Music by
JOHN WILLIAMS

Majestically, steady march (♩ = 108)

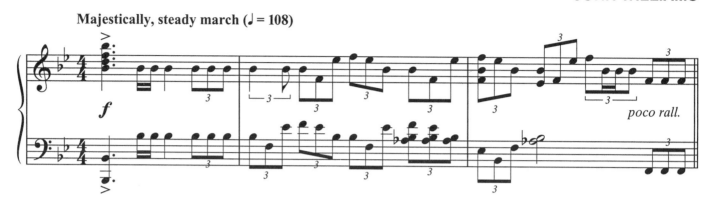

Star Wars - 4 - 1
PFM0513

ANAKIN'S BETRAYAL

Music by
JOHN WILLIAMS

Sorrowful (♩ = 72)

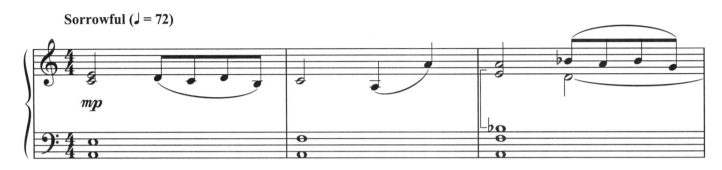

mp

(with pedal)

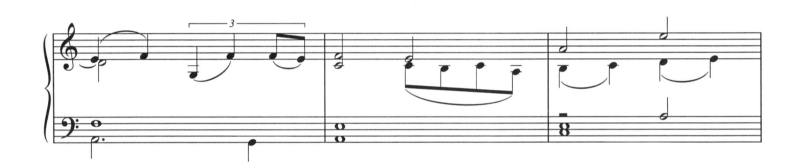

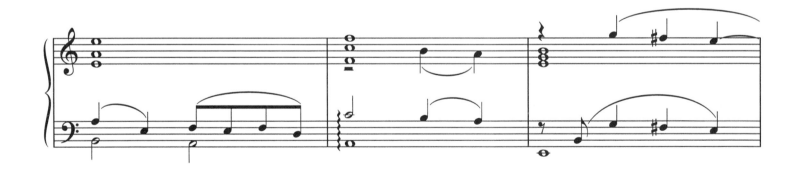

Anakin's Betrayal - 4 - 1
PFM0513

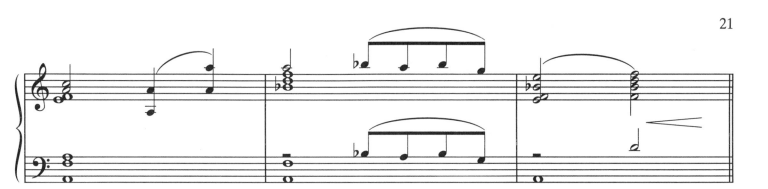

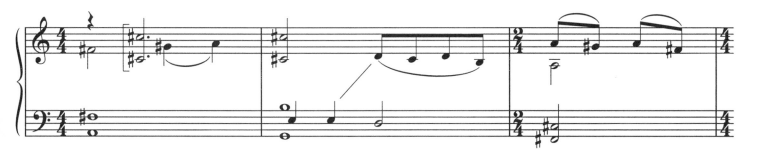

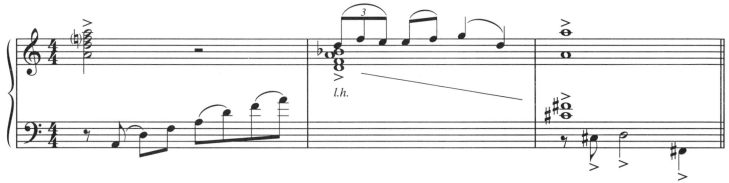

PADMÉ'S RUMINATIONS

Music by
JOHN WILLIAMS

Ominously (♩ = 80)

Padmé's Ruminations - 2 - 1
PFM0513

THE IMPERIAL MARCH
(Darth Vader's Theme)

Music by
JOHN WILLIAMS

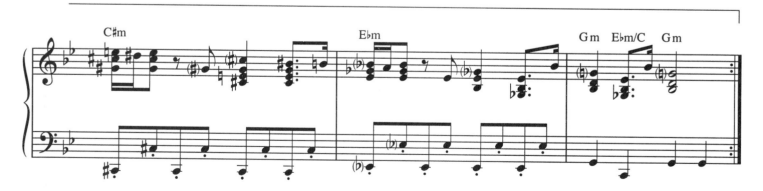

The Imperial March - 2 - 1
PFM0513

ANAKIN'S DARK DEEDS

Music by
JOHN WILLIAMS

Funereal (♩ = 63)

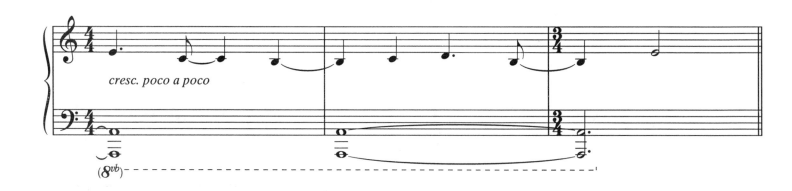

Viciously (♩ = 84)

Solemn

PADMÉ'S DESTINY

Music by
JOHN WILLIAMS

PRINCESS LEIA'S THEME

Music by
JOHN WILLIAMS

With a gentle flow and straight-eighth feeling ($\quarternote$ = 72)

THE FORCE THEME

Music by
JOHN WILLIAMS

THE THRONE ROOM

Music by
JOHN WILLIAMS

Maestoso (♩ = 112)

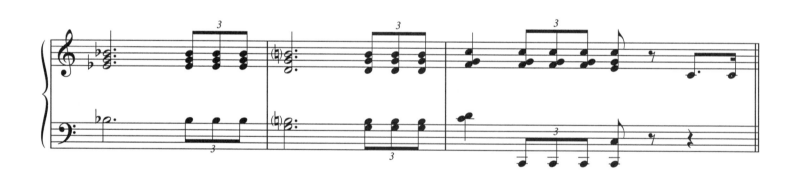

The Throne Room - 3 - 1
PFM0513

Poco meno mosso